THE HUGE SECRET BEHIND BEING SINGLE

WHAT YOU MUST DISCOVER BEFORE CHANGING YOUR STATUS

Shaun D. Upshaw

The Huge Secret Behind Being Single

What You Must Discover Before Changing Your Status

©Copyright 2016

Shaun D. Upshaw

Editor: Kendra Upshaw

For information regarding special discounts for bulk purchases, please contact mrupshaw2u@gmail.com

ACKNOWLEDGEMENTS

As always, I would like to first and foremost dedicate this book to my family. I would like to acknowledge my wife Kendra, my daughter Londin-Taylor, and my mother Dartha. Without your patience, love, support, and will to always stay proud of me, I would not be in position to author any books or do anything that revolves around walking in my purpose. So, I thank you! Next, I would like to thank the loyal supporters of Shaun D. Upshaw as a person and brand. I can never express enough gratitude for all the phone calls to encourage me to keep striving and the appearances at whatever I am involved in to show your support. Last, but certainly not least, I would like to thank God. I thank God for awakening within me everything I tried to keep sleep in order to avoid failure. Thank you for removing the fears, stumbling blocks, and people that stood in my way of greatness!

TABLE OF CONTENTS

PREFACE

For many of you this book is a last resort! It is the final straw to pull at finding a real reason as to why you believe to be single! And although many of you would love to believe that being single is a curse, I am here to inform you that in fact it is the total opposite. But, the only way I can get you on board with believing such a theory is by first convincing you with this book that a secret behind being single really does exist.

So now the question becomes, "Can you be sold on the idea that a secret behind being single does exist?" Yes! No! Maybe? Either way, I am going to share my expertise with you about singleness so that you hopefully can see what you need to see before thinking about changing your single status once again without a purpose behind it. But, before any of that can transpire, I know there are some preliminary questions floating around your mind for me to answer. I know that because most single people are skeptics when picking up a book concerning being single. With that said, allow me to make you a believer! Let me take a stab at some of the questions I think you might be thinking at the moment.

(Q 1) Why do you believe there is a secret behind being single?

I believe there is a huge secret behind being single because I personally have experienced the process. I personally have seen the results of those who I have given the secret. Not to mention, I personally believe in the strategy you will be using throughout this book to discover the huge secret behind being single. I really feel that the strategy will uncover an individual within yourself capable of removing your single status permanently, which means reaching an ultimate goal of an ultimate commitment whether it's through marriage or just something long term. But, that is just my opinion. Of course, you would have to read this book cover to cover to see if there is any accuracy in my beliefs.

(Q 2) What makes you so confident this huge secret can help me?

I believe this secret can help you because I mentally know where some of you presently are with regards to relationships and comprehend where some of you are heading in the future with regards to relationships if something revealing does not occur soon. Not only that, but I also comprehend the root of why most of you simply miss out on discovering this huge secret. One part of my root for understanding your lack of comprehension stems from knowing that majority of you would rather use being single as a pass to explore potential candidates for relationships than an opportunity to explore self for revelation. The other part of my root for understanding your lack of comprehension stems from knowing that majority of you just do not care to discover any secrets behind being single. You just want to be in a relationship, which by the way is no benefit to you or the person that you will choose for a relationship! So, to simply answer your initial question, lets just say I have an inside track of what you possibly are experiencing at the present moment.

(Q 3) What do you expect me to gain from this book?

I expect you to gain a better understanding of your present identity as a single person! I expect you to gain a better understanding of what your future identity can become as a single person! But most important, I expect you to gain from this book a better understanding of your thinking and actions as a single person, which will lead to understanding the huge secret behind you being single. What it comes down to is I want to show you how to humble yourself before future loneliness does it for you. Nothing more! Nothing less!

Are you ready to take the journey?

AND SO THE JOURNEY BEGINS...

By show of hands, how many of you have been **SINGLE** for so long that you have begin to wonder if something is wrong with you? How many of you have inquired why it appears everyone is in a relationship except you? How many of you have even questioned if relationships are for you? Seriously, how many of you are haunted by these thoughts or similar ones?

It's okay to admit it! You have no reason to be ashamed! Matter of fact, you should know that openly admitting to something being possibly wrong with you is groundbreaking! You should know that openly admitting to everyone possibly appearing to be in a relationship except you is refreshing! Moreover, you should know that openly admitting to feeling like relationships not possibly being for you at this particular moment show signs of growth! How?

First of all, it symbolizes that you are prepared to discover something about you. You are finally ready to dig deep into finding out the **"WHY"** behind your single status. Second, it means that you are prepared to correct the one big mistake you make as a single person. Last, but certainly not least, it means that you have officially and unconsciously come to grips with understanding the importance of timing. You merely want to see and understand the bigger picture behind being single now, which I can totally understand! So check this out!

The moment you reach a point of being prepared to discover something about yourself becomes the moment you officially give an open mind to a theory other than your own as to why you are single. It ultimately means you are prepared to learn as a single person **how to properly market yourself** for a relationship. Market myself? Yes! Whether you know it or not, the way you **market yourself** has a lot to do with you being single. Let me explain!

Marketing Yourself

People choose you as a potential partner based on what you show them and vice versa. You choose people as a potential partner based on what a person shows you. The reality of this situation is that majority of the things you do as a single person and what others do as single people to so-call maintain a "lifestyle" are in fact things done to unconsciously make the persona appear more marketable. (E.g., buying expensive vehicles, clothes, houses, fake nails, fake hair, etc.)

Now of course, most of you will argue my point. You will then support your argument by saying those things were purchased simply because "You like nice things" and "You like looking nice." But then again, some of you might be thinking and saying, "Well, if that is the case then what is wrong with maintaining a lifestyle Shaun?" My answer to you would be there absolutely is nothing wrong with it, especially if you like being pursued based on what you can bring to the table from a physical and materialistic standpoint. However, if you want a real answer that points out the real problem then let me give it to you.

The real problem with "Marketing Yourself" from just a physical and materialistic standpoint is that your focus will always center on how to better the exterior of you, which in turn will cause you to neglect improving on the interior of you. And although the physical and materialistic side of you will do a great job with finding you a relationship, in the end, it primarily will be the mental side of you that keeps the relationship in tact.

Does any of that make sense? In my mind, it makes perfect sense because when you learn the importance of how to **properly market yourself** as a single person, then it pushes you to want more for yourself. It forces you to look beyond what physical and materialistic elements can bring you. It calls for you to realize the mistakes that you make as a single person by solely marketing yourself in a physical and materialistic way. But more important, it positions you to see one of the biggest mistakes you make as a single person. Do you want to know that mistake?

Your Biggest Mistake

A single person's biggest mistake is **wasting time** and here is how majority of you do it. You waste time by jumping from relationship to relationship without learning anything about yourself in between the failure of those relationships. For example, when you have only "**marketed yourself**" from a physical and materialistic standpoint, then you miss out on discovering the real reason why those types of relationships often fail. How? Most of you miss out on the discovery because instead of taking time to learn how to **properly market yourself** in between the failure of those types of relationships, you unconsciously focus on upgrading what you believe your last relationship lacked.

Now, if you can not see the big mistake in carrying that state of mind around with you, then my questions to you are: What have you improved on as a single person from your last courting relationship experience? What have you learned about yourself as a single person that will make you ready for the next one? What will you do differently to address the challenges in a new courting relationship once those challenges arrive?

Here is the reality! You will not improve as a single person! You will not learn anything about yourself as a single person that prepares you for another courting relationship. Lastly, you will address new challenges in your new relationship in the same manner as you addressed challenges in the old ones. Why? Here are the reasons!

Reason One: It would be hard for you to improve as a single person, especially when your focus would be on pointing the finger of blame at your ex. Why would your focus be on pointing the finger of blame at your ex? It is because when you are caught up with **marketing yourself** in a physical and materialistic way then you start to believe that everything you physically and materialistically brought into your previous relationship should have been good enough to sustain it. Your focus solely remains on how unappreciative you believe your ex partners were in those particular relationships rather than focusing on what you could improve on as a single individual.

Reason Two: It would be tough for you to prepare yourself for another courting relationship when you unconsciously will be always searching for a possible upgrade. What does that mean? The bottom line is when you choose to only **market yourself** in a physical and materialistic way, then you miss out on the opportunity while being single to upgrade the most important thing about yourself, which is your way of thinking and actions. The reason you miss out on such an opportunity is simple! You unconsciously become more caught up with trying to upgrade to a partner that you think would fall to your feet in admiration due to what you are physically and materialistically bringing into the relationship rather than improving on what matters most, which is your mentality toward relationships.

Reason Three: It would just be difficult to address challenges in a new relationship when all you did was mishandle challenges in the previous ones. How did you mishandle challenges in previous relationships? You mishandled those challenges by not challenging yourself enough to see yourself in the problems that were brought to you in those previous relationships. As stated earlier, when you choose to only market yourself in a physical and materialistic way then your focus centers on the exterior rather than interior, which makes it tough for you to take on the necessary self-examination.

Reason Four: Hate to say it, but you just do not have the slightest clue of who you are presently and who you want to be in the future. I feel one of the reasons you are unaware of the present and future of yourself is because as previously stated you simply do not give yourself enough time to figure how you should properly market yourself. With you not giving yourself enough time to learn that element of being single, then that means the timing of all your future courting relationships will be off. Not to mention, you will continuously fail to see the true benefits of having a relationship, which eventually will fuel every negative thought that you currently have about being single.

Is any of this making sense to you? Well again, in my mind it is making perfect sense because once you realize the importance of **properly marketing yourself** and realize **the big mistake** that stems from not doing it, then you comprehend the significance of timing. You begin to realize that there are just certain elements in which you are suppose to encounter as a single person that requires time to completely grasp it. You start to realize that there is just no other way to complete this process. You start to understand why going through this timing process is the one element that points out a key purpose behind being single. To sum this up in a few words, timing is everything and here is why.

Timing

Have you ever broken up with someone only to realize the reason for your breakup was bad timing? The person was everything you wanted and needed, but the timing of their arrival was just wrong. It happens all the time, but why? One reason is because you are not giving yourself enough time to learn from your mistakes between breakups as previously stated. The next reason is you just do not take a closer look at the type of people drawn to you through your way of marketing yourself, which basically means the law of attraction is very real! So what are you saying here Shaun?

I am saying that most of the people that you've had bad relationships with were drawn to you based on whatever you were selling yourself as at that particular moment! In other words, the wasted time jumping from bad relationship to relationship is what eventually leads to the mistiming of the relationships that you actually were supposed to be in. Now, do I put the entire blame on you? No! However, I do put the responsibility of discovering an alternative way of how to market yourselves outside of the physical and materialistic way on you. I do put the responsibility of getting your timing together!

The reason I am placing those responsibilities on you is because ultimately you are missing out on obtaining the long-term commitments that most of you desire. You are missing out on discovering what you need to find out before changing your single status again. You basically are missing out on discovering the huge secret behind being single and it all boils down to bad timing, a big mistake, and an improper way of marketing yourself. So, what do you have to say for yourself?

I really want you to seriously think about that question because essentially you have been robbing yourself of a purposeful experience. You have been missing the opportunity to improve as a single person with a goal of one day being apart of a lasting relationship or opportunity to accomplish whatever particular goals you have in mind as a single person. You have been selling yourself short, but that is over now. The reason that's over is because you have taken the first step by selecting this book to read.

In my opinion, I believe this book will point you in the right direction of finding a solution as to why you are single. You just have to be honest with yourself along this journey to see if what is being read resonates something within you to want change in how you operate as a single person. My only request is that you keep an open mind. Give my theory on how to improve your way of thinking and acting as a single person a fighting chance! I ask that you take each process seriously. More significantly, ask yourself the important questions at the end of this book, which are what did I learn about myself? How can I improve as a single person now?

So, without further ado, here is my insight on how you can learn to **"properly market yourself"** and how you can learn to uncover the huge secret behind being single. Enjoy!

THE GUIDE

Now that you are onboard with understanding the significance behind properly marketing yourself, we can move on to the next phase of this process. I can now reveal the steps that need to be taken to discover the huge secret behind being single. Having stated that, let's start with the first and most important aspect that kicks off this discovery, which is **THE GUIDE!**

So, I am about to step out on a limb here! I am going to say that most of you do not have a clue of your identity as a single person at this particular stage of being single. Simply put, the reason is I feel you have allowed outside influences to create that identity for you. But hold on, I am not finish stepping out...

I'm also going to say that not having a clue of your identity is the very thing preventing you from being the single person that you really want to be at this particular stage. And since I am already standing far out on that limb, let me finish by saying that most of you probably do not even have any inclination of where to begin the process of finding out your present identity; nor how to become the identity that you really want to be. But, have no fear because that is the purpose of this guide. It kick starts the process.

So, my first question out the gates is have you ever heard of a mission and vision statement? I am sure most of you have or have some type a clue about it. But I'm also willing to bank on most of you not knowing the definition or purpose behind either statement, which is why I am going to explain it anyway. The dictionary defines a mission statement as, "a formal summary of the aims and values of a company, organization, or **individual**." That is the technical definition of a mission statement, but here is the definition that I want you to define it as for the sake of this book. **A mission statement is primarily an overview of your present state of mind as a single person.**

Now, as far as a vision statement, the technical definition is "an organization's declaration of its mid-term and long-term goals." However, here is the definition that I want you to define it as for the sake of this book. **A vision statement is a goal of where you really want to be as a single person.** Please be sure to keep these definitions in mind because you will need them to accurately complete and understand the purpose of this section. Another reason is I will be asking you to write down your personal mission and vision statement. Why? It is because you need to know **where you presently are mentally with regards to being single and where you want to be**

in the future with regards to being single. But before we can even think about heading in that direction, I have rules to throw out there for you with regards to creating your personal mission and vision statement.

Ground Rules

❖ When creating your mission statement be truthful about your present state of mind as a single person whether you hurt, bitter, angry, or etc.

❖ When creating your vision statement be truthful about where you would like to be as a single person despite the hurt, bitterness, anger, or etc.

❖ Do not to sugarcoat anything

❖ Make sure there is plenty of accountability in each statement

❖ Please do not forget this process is for you and not anybody else (In other words, dig deep for your responses and worry less about what others would say about your answers)

There are my rules for creating your personal mission and vision statements ladies and gentlemen! To better assist you with this process and every other process throughout this book, I will provide you with my personal step-by-step playbook of everything I had written in each process beginning with my personal mission and vision statement. I hope my personal statements help you with clarifying what your statements should look like for this exercise. Let's get started!

> **Mission Statement:** To get everything I want out of someone without giving anything in return that places me in a position of vulnerability, hurt, and/or brokenness.

> **Vision Statement:** To become a person who can love someone in freedom! Freedom from past hurts! Freedom from brokenness! Freedom from bitterness! Freedom of unforgiveness! Freedom from self-sabotaging! Freedom from victimization! Freedom from familiarity (Characteristics that were unconsciously inherited from my parent's relationship experiences)

Now, if you are wondering how I came up with those statements then I would be glad tell you. I honestly submitted myself to being upfront about my true identity at the particular time I started this process. Then I honestly submitted myself to being upfront about the true identity of who I really wanted to be at the end of this process. I would be lying if I stated this was an easy process. Let's be honest here! Who really wants to admit to being messed up? Who really wants to admit to being in a terrible state of mind? Who really wants to admit that they are not the person claimed to be?

This was extremely challenging for me. However, it was not more challenging than putting on a constant front of pretending to be a single person that was ready for a courting relationship when in reality I was far from ready. That was a challenge within itself! So, how about you allow that to sink in your thoughts for a moment? I mean really let it sink in as you prepare to be completely honest about your present state of mind as a single person. I mean really let it sink in as you prepare to be completely honest about the person you would really love to be as a single person. Are you ready? There is no better time than now to take a stand against everything you have been doing wrong as a single person. All you have to do is submit to the truth about you! So, let's start with the most significant part of this process first, which is the mission statement. Let's get to writing!

Personal Mission Statement

_____

_____

_____

_____

_____

_____

Well, congratulations! You have just completed the very first phase in the process of discovering the huge secret behind being single. How do you feel about what you have written down? Were you brutally honest with yourself regarding where you presently are as a single person? I surely hope so because it is the only way that you can accurately create your vision statement. It is honesty about where you are now that gives you opportunity to accept honest direction toward where you want to be in the future.

Do not sell yourself short of a self-discovering experience all because you refuse to be truthful about the ugliness within you at this particular moment. Just accept the opportunity to be honest. After all, you want to get phase one right because phase two is an important phase. It is important because phase two deals with your true identity. It is the phase that resurrects the person you truly are at heart. It is the phase that reveals the authentic and genuine nature of who you would like to be as a single person.

So, to create your vision statement, all you have to do now is be honest about your true identity minus your present state of mind. The reason I was so certain about my vision was because I knew the person associated with my vision would be better prepared for the long-term commitment that I desired as a single person. The same applies for you. You just have to move aside the pride, insecurities, past hurt, and any other distractions that could be possibly preventing you from writing down what is truly inside in your heart to be as a single person. You have to write down the vision of the person who would be better prepared for the desired long-term commitment that you desire. So lets give it a shot!

Personal Vision Statement

_____

_____

_____

_____

_____

Once again, congratulations! You have just completed phase two of the guide that helps you discover the huge secret behind being single. The question probably roaming around your mind now is what's next? Or something a little more logical such as what really was the purpose of writing down those statements? Both questions are fair to ask and here are the answers. The purpose of writing down those statements outside of the explanation rendered earlier in the section was for you to recognize something important.

I wanted you to see on paper the constant war that goes on between the individual you have allowed your past to create as a single person versus the individual your heart really wants you to be as a single person. I wanted you to see on paper that there is a choice to make with regards to what can rule your thoughts and actions as a single person. But more significantly, I wanted to give you the first secret to uncovering the huge secret behind being single just in case you needed an incentive as to why you should continue with this process.

I want you to consider what you've just written down as your launching point. I want you to consider it your launching point because there is no way that you can mentally return to where you were as a single person now, especially after discovering what you just discovered about yourself. You have officially taken yourself to another level. Confessing where you mentally are presently and where you want to mentally be in the future now places you with an advantage. It now gives you insight into figuring out your situation a little better. But in all honesty, my hope is that it intrigues you to want to hear a strategy on how to actually reflect your vision and stay consistent with reflecting it.

Having stated that, let's move on to the next step of the process!

THE STRATEGY

With just about everything in life, you need a strategy to have any type of success. The same applies for single people with a vision to be the single person that their heart desires them to be. The point here is if you do not have a strategy on how to become the person your vision reflects, then you will not discover any secrets behind being single. You will just continue to look at being single in the same fashion, as you always have looked at it, which is in false reality. Unfortunately, I had to learn this lesson the hard way. Fortunately, this book will not allow you to experience my journey prior to this process. With that stated, let me give you my spiel on why I feel a strategy helps you reach your vision more effectively.

- **Reason One:** Strategy uncovers your real strengths and shows you how those real strengths contribute to becoming who you really are (**Vision Statement**)
- **Reason Two:** Strategy reveals the true purpose behind weaknesses and why those weaknesses contribute to your present state of mind (**Mission Statement)**
- **Reason Three:** Strategy shows the difference between real opportunity

for a serious courting relationship vs. the opportunity you often take to be an opportunist for a relationship

- **Reason Four:** Strategy points out the threats associated with choosing to operate as a single person from your personal Mission Statement **(Present State Of Mind)** and other elements versus your personal Vision Statement (**Where you really want to be**)

Do any of these reasons strike your interest as to why strategy is significant? I would hope so because that is what it comes down to if you really want to discover this huge secret behind being single. You must employ a strategy that reveals a plan on how to reflect your vision. Once you come to grips with understanding this is how the process works, it becomes easier to get into position of receiving that fulfilling relationship or ultimate goal as a single person that you have desired. So, let's talk about this strategy a little more. Let's talk about how it was introduced to me. Let's talk about why I chose to use it in spite of its original purpose.

The Strategy

This strategy that I used to help me reach my vision and eventually unlock the huge secret behind being single has been around for quite a while. It was actually introduced to me in a business marketing class. Now, I know some of you at this moment are probably scratching your heads in confusion and looking at this book with skepticism asking, "How did a business marketing class help you with your personal life?" How did it assist you with discovering some huge secret behind being single? So, let me answer those questions for you.

I gave a breakdown earlier of the significance behind learning how to properly market you, but now it is time to get a little more elaborate. It is time for me to share "the how and why" I believe a simple business marketing strategy pushed me into being bold enough to believe in everything I have told you to this point. It is time for me to escort you into my reasoning as to why a strategy just made sense for me to use in my personal life.

Have you heard of a SWOT analysis? If not, let me give you my definition before I give you the technical one. A SWOT analysis is the key element that saved me from destroying my chances for a successful relationship. What do you mean by that Shaun? I mean this SWOT analysis gave me a better comprehension of why I was single. It rendered me insight into how I was marketing myself, who I was marketing myself to for relationship courting attention, and what I should concentrate more on to market myself the proper way. But more important, this SWOT analysis showed me how to get naked. Not literally, but figuratively, which I will explain later.

Nevertheless, if you are searching for a technical definition of a SWOT analysis then let me provide it. The dictionary defines a SWOT analysis as, "a study undertaken by an organization to identify its internal strengths and weaknesses, as well as the organization's internal & external opportunities and threats." Basically, the reason an organization would use a SWOT analysis is to determine the strengths and weaknesses of the organization. Then it would determine the advantage it has or could gain over its **competitor** through examining the organization's opportunities and threats. There are many ways to describe a SWOT, but that is the general version. Well Shaun, if that is the technical definition then how does this apply to me? Who would be considered the competitor in this case?

To be quite frank, your biggest competitor is you. Whether you know it or not, you are always competing with yourself. Not just you as individual per say, but with everything that you have learned up to this point regarding being single that has tainted and prevented you from exploring the authentic reason behind why you really are single. Now, I know some of you are still wondering how does this SWOT analysis coincide with being single? Or, how does this help change your single status? So, please allow me to give you another case and point as to why I am pushing this SWOT strategy so tough. Let me give you a personal, yet controversial relationship theory of mine that hopefully shines some light on my point and gets us on the same page. Here we go!

I, Shaun D. Upshaw wholeheartedly believe that individuals and businesses are similar in some ways. Now, I have been shot down before by having such a theory, but hear me out before you shoot it down with your negativity and attempt to poke holes in it. Just give this theory of mine a chance before you say something like, "There are too many emotional factors that can separate businesses and individuals." Or "How does one compare to the other?"

In fact, do yourself a favor and simply ask me, "how are individuals and businesses similar?" And here is the answer to that great question! First, individuals and businesses are similar because they are two entities. Second, individuals and businesses are similar because they are two entities that desire to reach a goal. The individual among many other goals has a bottom line goal of one day finding someone to share a fulfilling life with whereas a business among many other goals has a bottom line goal of discovering ways to create longevity as well as success. With that stated, the real commonality between individuals and businesses is both need a **strategy** for reaching their specific bottom line goal. But, here is where the problem lies!

In most cases, the business will know or discover a way to know what has to be done to reach their bottom line goal. But, as for the individual, he/she will not know, he/she will not find a way to know, and he/she will somehow trick themselves into believing that not knowing is a benefit. In fact, he/she will go as far as mistaking not knowing how to reach their bottom line goal into a false sense of believing that it is simply not meant for them to know it at that particular moment. The "know" of how to reach their goal will magically just come with the experience of life. So, my response to those people is, "that is a bunch of crap" and my question to those people is "How many break ups will it take for you to realize that not knowing is one of the main roots of your problem?"

Here is what I am basically saying to you ladies and gents. Stop bamboozling yourself! Stop tricking yourself into believing experience will be the best teacher when in reality you can identify the problems yourself that lead to you being single by simply implementing a strategy to discover it. You just have to make it an honest priority to do it rather than wait on experience to teach something that you should already know about yourself. You have to want to reach your bottom-line goal of finding someone to share a fulfilling life with people and that is what this SWOT analysis will give you and more!

I know many of you believe right now this strategy sounds insane and has nothing to do with being single. But, I believe it does not sound any less insane than you believing in any of the other stuff people try telling you works. What it boils down to is everyone has a good, bad, and ugly that resides within him/her. For you to discover what that good, bad, and ugly is then you must be willing to expose yourself. You must be willing to expose yourself in a way where opinions of others no longer matter. You must be willing to expose yourself in a way that removes all your old ways of thinking, saying, and doing as a single person. You must be willing to get naked!

In my opinion, the only way to get naked is by using a single person's SWOT analysis to show you what getting naked can do for you as a single person. Using this SWOT analysis as your strategy to help you reach and reflect your vision is the best way to do it. I can say that because my single person's SWOT analysis helped me become the person I set out to be. It helped me find my good, my bad, and my ugly while showing me how to use the information it revealed to my benefit of reaching my vision. I believe the same results can happen for you! You just have to be willing to try something extraordinary to achieve it!

As I stated in the Preface, for many of you this book is a last straw. This is all you have left to pull when it comes to figuring everything out. If I may say so myself, I think you are pulling the right straw by using this strategy. After all, I am not asking for your first-born kids here. I am just asking that you attempt to use something capable of helping you find the type of love you desire and deserve. All I am asking is for you to trust the process! See what it unlocks about you! Watch what it does to mentally improve you as a single person. Then, just go from there!

Now, lets move into discussing the strategy secrets that are supposed lead you to the promised land of discovering the huge secret behind being single.

STRATEGY SECRET #1

The first thing a single person's SWOT analysis wants to reveal about you is your strengths. But, before the great reveal can occur, my question is how many of you actually know your strengths? And I am not referring to that list of strengths that you believe are strengths! I am talking about your **real strengths**. Do you have a clue of what those might be?

There is that limb again for me to step back out on it ladies and gents. So, let me step back out on it to say the answer is no and please understand that I am not being cynical in any kind of way. It actually is the experience of witnessing many of you fail as single people seeking a courting relationship rendering the answer. It also is the fact of me knowing that your failure is a mere result of **"You Just Not Knowing Your Real Strengths"** which is totally cool. So with that being the case, how does the misfortunate of **"Not Knowing Your Real Strengths"** happen?

The explanation is simple yet complex! Here are my thoughts on the matter! The reason you do not know your real strengths is because you have unconsciously chosen to highlight your qualities as strengths. The reason you chose to pinpoint qualities as strengths is because qualities makes you appear more marketable for a relationship. But, what you fail to realize is being more marketable for a relationship does not necessarily make you ready for one. In fact, the qualities that you have coined as strengths are the elements that have clouded your judgment and slowed your process of becoming the single person that your vision statement reflects. If you beg to differ with that theory, then answer this one question before you shut me down.

Why are the strengths that you believe to be strengths not helping you to sustain any of your courting relationships?

Now, before you run down a million and one excuses as to why none of your courting relationships have not sustained, allow me to provide you the answer to that question. I promise that it is really straight to the point! The answer is nothing or nobody has pushed you to a point of digging deep enough to understand what your real strengths are as of yet, which is why I am here and why this book is in your hands. It is to show you what real strengths are and what real strengths are not. Check this list out!

Basic Things People Classify As Strengths

Listening Skills
Communication Skills
Providing Abilities
Nurturing Abilities
Love Making Abilities (Sex)

Now of course there could be more, but I just wanted to give you these five basic ones that most of you tend to believe are strengths. In fact, I can say with confidence that at one point or another one of those five if not all has been labeled by you as strengths when asked the question, "What are your strengths as a person?" The reason I adamantly believe you have used these elements is because I literally have heard majority of you run down that identical list when asked the question, "What makes you an attractive candidate for a relationship?" And I really hate to be the one that burst your bubble with reality, but everything on that list most of you have been claiming as strengths are nothing more than **learned qualities**.

Yes! You heard me correctly! Everything listed on that list is considered in my book a **learned quality**. Learned quality? What is a **learned quality**? A **learned quality** is a quality that anyone willing to learn can learn if that person desires to have that particular quality apart of his/her make-up. It means if your learned quality is being a great listener, then somewhere down the lines you decided to pick up, **learn**, and make a part of your make-up the art of how to be a great listener. **But, here is the kicker ladies and gentlemen!**

That learned quality is not your real strength! Why? Let me tell you! First, it does not give you any distinct differentiation from anyone else. But, outside of that obvious reason, here are the differences between learned qualities and real strengths. My hope is that after you read the difference that it places you and I on the same page throughout the remaining of this section. That way I can get you one step closer to figuring out why uncovering **real strengths** instead of focusing on **learned qualities** is the strategy secret that kicks off the initiative toward changing your single status forever.

Learned Qualities versus Real Strengths

"Learned Qualities" are merely features about you that make you appear more marketable to other people looking for someone to compliment their features. It basically means on paper you have the potential to **appear** perfect for a relationship. But, there is a catch! The catch is learned qualities without knowledge of real strengths cannot sustain a relationship.

"**Strengths**" are what makes you as an individual strong. Strengths are the very foundation of you. Strengths are what you bring to the table as a single person that makes you different from another single person. Unlike a learned quality, strengths can solely sustain a relationship. Or at least sustain it long enough until you comprehend which learned qualities are supposed to mix with a particular real strength to sustain it.

That is basically the difference between learned qualities and real strengths. If that explanation still has you a little unsure of the difference between the two, then check this out. Hopefully what I'm about to tell you will make it even clearer for you! Just read these next few lines carefully! Learned qualities can help with your **search** for **a** relationship as a single person. However, it is your real strengths that will **place** you in **the** relationship that you desire as a single person. In my opinion, there is a big difference with being in just "**A Relationship**" versus being in "**The Relationship.**" And I'm willing to bet at this point of your singleness that you are looking for "**The Relationship**."

I am also willing to bet that you believe you deserve **"The Relationship"** as well. So, what I am going to do next is provide you with an opportunity just as I did in the guide section of this book. But, this time I need you to jot down what you know to be your real strengths. I need you to write down what you believe to be the foundations of you!

The reason I want you to write all that down is because it moves you closer toward finding **"The Relationship"** that you desire. It also gives you a better understanding of why learned qualities mixed with real strengths is the real reason relationships sustain. But, for those of you not sure of what your real strengths are then do not fret. Like before, I will use myself as an example of what you should be looking for within yourself to write down as real strengths. I will give you the foundation of me that will hopefully help you discover the foundation of you. Here we go!

Shaun Upshaw's Real Strengths
Individuality
Loyalty
Unconditional Love

I know some of you are probably looking at my list and saying to yourself, "Is that it Shaun?" You just gave us a huge presentation on the importance of knowing your real strengths only to name three. Trust me, I know what you are thinking. But, what I need you to know is the length of your list is irrelevant. The only thing significant to think about at this point is, "Does the list reflect the foundation of me?" My list does that ladies and gentlemen and your list should reflect the foundation of you as well. Why? It is because you need to be sure as a single person that your foundation is solid before you attempt to build something with someone. There is nothing worst then attempting to build something with someone from a shaky foundation of who you are as a single person. That relationship would be scheduled for destruction in no time.

With that stated, lets take a detour right here before I get you to writing down anything. I want to take this specific time to explain what gives you an indication that something could be considered your real strength or foundation of you. I want you to have as much insight as possible into figuring out this process of what your real strengths might be, which is the purpose of this detour. Before we move on, please remember that this exercise is to inform you of what you actually bring to the table as a single person instead of assuming it. Here is the real strength indicator!

The moment you reach a point, as a single person where you can **master** certain aspects of your life becomes the moment those aspects transform into strengths. For example, individuality was named as one of my strengths. Why? It was named one of my strengths because I learned to **master** it.

By learning to master individuality, I learned how to see people as individuals rather than experiences that generalized them. Meaning, I was able to learn how to deal with individuals based on who they were rather than whom I believed them to be. That alone, put me in position to realize that everything that starts out the same will not end the same. What do you mean by that Shaun?

Here is what I mean! One of the main reasons I was unable to elevate my single status to a relationship status was because I would always generalize people based on familiarity. Meaning, a trigger of sabotage would go off the very moment I saw someone new doing something someone old had done to me in a prior experience. I basically would end any potential relationship before it even started simply because of an assumed result. At that time, I did not fully understand that just because something starts out appearing one way that it could possibly end in another way. I merely was judging people based on familiarity of past situations rather than the individuality of that person.

Once I learned the benefit of mastering individuality, it helped me transition into a relationship much easier. It also helped me uncover that individuality was one of my strengths. It was a foundation within me. Anyone who knows me personally knows that I constantly harp on breaking from the mold of society and being your own individual. It is one of the cornerstones of my purpose. Now, I know some of you might not understand that, but it is okay. I do not expect you to understand it. Why?

Not everyone will have, nor understand the strength of having individuality as a personal foundation. That is the reason why! In fact, understanding that everyone is not equipped with the strength of individuality is what helped me comprehend what I brought to the table as a single person. Ding! Ding! Ding! And guess what? The same will happen for you once you figure out your real strengths! Once you figure out the cornerstones of your purpose, it is then and only then will you figure out which learned quality to mix with your real strength to not just sustain a relationship, but also take it to the next level.

For example, one of my learned qualities was listening. With individuality being one of my real strengths, I now was able to use my learned quality of listening in the proper way. I now was in a position to listen to any potential issue my mate could have with me without prejudice. I really could begin to hear the exact messages that were trying to be conveyed. I now could properly judge a person's intentions based on them as an individual rather then generalizing them based on a prior experience.

In a nutshell, I finally understood why individuality was one of my strengths. It was to better myself as a single person and hopefully better anyone that I encountered who might not have it as one of their strengths. I learned that it was what I brought to the table as a balance to anyone who lacked it. From there, it literally became so simple to understand what the rest of my strengths were as a single person. Once that indicator was revealed, I begin to adapt a mentality that sparked something to carry with me on my single journey.

Here is what it sparked: **I learned that "Strong Foundation" as an individual makes an even "Stronger Individual In A Relationship." It taught me that there is no way a relationship can hold steadfast if the individuals in it do not have a clue of what makes them strong as individuals first.**

Okay, so that is enough with all my philosophies and examples! Let's get to the purpose of this section! Lets get to writing down some of your real strengths! For some strange reason I feel you are up to the task now! Remember, all you have to do is think about what is natural about you and symbolizes the foundation of you. Here is your opportunity to do that ladies and gentlemen. Have at it!

THE HUGE SECRET BEHIND BEING SINGLE

Personal Strengths

_____

_____

_____

_____

_____

Congratulations! I knew you could you do it! I am very proud of you at this moment! My only hope is that you were just as honest about your real strengths as you were about your mission and vision statement. If you recall, I stated the only way you can come close to being a reflection of your vision statement is through pure honesty. I hate to keep reminding you of that, but I will until you get it! I also hate to keep reminding you that this is nobody's process but yours, but I will until you get it!

You must comprehend that this is your time to step up and be who you envision to be as a single person. You can no longer use being hurt as an excuse! You can no longer use having trust issues as an excuse! You just have to be transparent about who you really are in order to shed the shadows of who you really are not! There is no way you can continue to be an imposter ready for a successful relationship, especially if you are not clear about what makes you strong as a single person.

It is timeout for just claiming qualities that make you appear more marketable for a relationship. It is time in for discovering real strengths that make you actually ready for one. The purpose of this section is to uncover the raw materials that are needed for you to start building a real foundation. Once the foundation of "who you are" is constructed then it becomes clear as to what "**learned qualities**" can enhance you and help you become the single person your vision statement reflects.

Now, are you ready to discuss strategy secret #2? Let's do it!

STRATEGY SECRET #2

The next thing a **Single Person SWOT analysis** calls for you to reveal about you is your weaknesses. Are you ready to discuss that part of you? Are you prepared to face something that most of you love to avoid bringing up? But more important, are you open to accepting a theory as to why everything you believe about your weaknesses is the total opposite of what a weakness is defined as and purposed for in this case? If so, then let's get started!

Whether you believe this or not, your weaknesses have a definition! Your weaknesses have a purpose! There is a secret within your weaknesses that must be uncovered for you to gain direction on how to become the single person **that you envision to be**. One surefire way to unlock that secret is by letting go of this crutch that you have proudly stood on every time something does not go your way as a single person. Now, are you prepared to do that people? I know for some of you that might be a tough pill to swallow considering you have been using this crutch of weaknesses for a very long time. But, if you truly desire to get in position of becoming the single person **that you envision to be**, then that pill should not be that hard to swallow. So let's get to work!

The dictionary provides three definitions to define a weakness when you search it. Here are the three definitions:

- ✓ The **state** or **condition** of lacking strength

- ✓ A quality or feature regarded as a **disadvantage** or fault

- ✓ A person or thing that one is **unable to resist** or likes excessively

Judging by those definitions, I can see why most of you avoid speaking on your weaknesses. After all, who wants to admit being associated with a word defined by those meanings? I wholeheartedly empathize with you! However, that does not mean I sympathize nor agree with you choosing to live comfortably behind your weaknesses. My consoling only goes but so far! Besides, I am not here to render you any sympathy or agreement anyway! I am here to take away those feelings of avoidance and comfort, which are some of the main reasons you use your weaknesses as a crutch in the first place. I am primarily here to help you understand the meaning and purpose of your weaknesses as well as give you the direction in which you supposed to go after acknowledging them. So, let's get started!

Do you recall in the "**Guide Section**" when I spoke about what you do as an individual when you do not know your bottom line goal of being single? Let me give it to you again just in case you don't remember it. Here is what I stated:

> He/she will undoubtedly make the mistake of transforming not knowing how to reach their bottom line goal into a false sense of believing that it is simply not meant for them to know at that particular moment. It is believed that the "know" of how to reach your goal will someday come with experience.

Now, of course you know there is a reason I wanted you to remember that particular part. The reason is there is a similarity in what you do when your bottom line goal is not clear as a single person and what you do when you are not aware of the definition as well as purpose behind your weaknesses as a single person. The similarity is **you transform your weaknesses into a false sense of believing**. Believing what? You transform it into believing that you can operate as a single person out of your weaknesses as long as you are up front and honest about it. I believe the term that many of you use to hide behind this neurotic way of thinking is "This is just who I am and people are going to have to accept it."

Well once again, you have been misinformed. Not to mention, you are making three vital mistakes with that type of mentality! The first mistake is thinking that people have to accept anything from you. The second mistake is thinking that way of thinking is acceptable. The third mistake is thinking your single status will somehow change by choosing that way of thinking rather than comprehending the definition, purpose, and direction in which your weaknesses are supposed to take you as a single person. Listen up!

The definition of a weakness is not to force people to accept it just because you are honest about it. The purpose behind a weakness is not to provide you a crutch to stand on in order for you to stay the same. Last, the direction of a weakness is most certainly not supposed to lead you into believing any of that nonsense. In fact, it's honesty about your weaknesses followed by correction that directs you toward accomplishing your vision of becoming the single person you desire to be. It actually is the definition and purpose that improves your chances of being directed to a place of becoming the single person you envision to be. Everything must work together just for you to comprehend the significance behind this secret.

So to answer the initial question, "What is the definition of a weakness?" I will say the definition of a weakness is just what was stated in the beginning of this section. But, allow me to make it even more concise for you. A weakness is a present **condition** that puts you at a **disadvantage** due to the fact that you cannot **resist** accepting that your **mental state of health** is unhealthy. So now when you ask the question, "What is the purpose of weakness?" I can say that the purpose of a weakness is to expose any **unhealthy mental states** that prevent you from operating within your real strengths, which in turn keeps you from becoming the single person that you envision to be. Now that you are aware of the definition and purpose of a weakness, the question now is, "Are you ready to get direction on how to get past those **unhealthy mental states** in order to concentrate on accomplishing your vision?"

There is that limb again! Allow me to step back out on it and say the answer is yes. I am even going to take a step further and assume that you are beyond ready to get direction now. Why? I do not know! For some reason, I just have this feeling that you want to release anything and everything that puts you in an **unhealthy mental state** now. Call me crazy, but I just have a feeling that you want to revaluate your current mission statement and really underline the origin of why your present state of mental health is unhealthy now. In fact, to prove it, I have provided you with yet another blank space that allows you to do exactly what I just stated. But like before, I will use me as an example first to make you feel comfortable with completing this process. As always, I hope it helps. Here you go!

Shaun Upshaw's Weaknesses or Conditions

Abandonment- I wrote about this in a previous book of mine entitled "Don't Be An Ass All Your Life." I wrote about how before coming to grips with realizing that my father not being in my life was no fault of mine, how I suffered from an abandonment **condition.** Needless to say, it had gotten so bad that I felt every partner I dealt with at some point would leave me. So, what I did to accommodate this condition was make myself emotionally unavailable. Basically, I would pass on using one of my real strengths in my relationships, which is emotional loyalty to allow my weakness of abandonment to take control.

During that time, I believed that I was merely exposing the inevitable before it transpired. However, the only thing being exposed during that time without being aware of it was my insecurities within myself. I was stuck in this condition of believing that no one had the ability to love or stick with me through thick and thin if my own father was incapable of doing it, which caused me to bury my real strengths and operate within in relationships from an unhealthy mental state. It was very bad! It was very, very bad! But, I think you get the point so let's move on to my next condition!

Self Sufficiency- Many of you would not consider being self-sufficient as a weakness or condition. However, if you exercise no balance with being self-sufficient as a single person, then it is sad to say but your state of health will be unhealthy for a relationship. Trust me! Let me explain it you!

At one point of being single, I had grown so self-sufficient that my belief became "If it was not done my way, then it most certainly was done the wrong way." In those moments, I figured it would be best to do everything on my own because trusting someone else to do it would only leave me with disappointment. **News Flash:** That type of self-sufficiency was wrong to have as a single person, especially a single person seeking a healthy relationship. Not only did it taint my definition of partnership, but also it caused me not to trust anything to anybody. It caused me to judge them based off prior results of past relationships versus the results that they could provide me in a relationship as an individual.

Doesn't that sound familiar? This condition provided me yet another reason not to use one of my real strengths. I allowed this weakness to be top dog instead of allowing my strengths to assume the position. This condition basically isolated me from ever considering trusting any of my relationship partners and at one point placed the question of, "Why do I even need a relationship?" in my mind.

So, as you can see my weaknesses directly affected how I was supposed to act in relationships. These conditions pushed me to focus on protecting my present state of mind, which was totally unhealthy rather than my vision. But more significantly, it pushed me further away from operating as a single person based on foundation. Now lets turn the focus back on you!

Like my strengths, as you can see I had very few conditions. But, I felt my conditions were the most dangerous. Why? In my opinion, I felt my conditions of abandonment and self-sufficiency had the power to couple with so many other conditions that could have stockpiled on top of my unhealthy state of health. Now of course, I know some of you might beg to differ, but as I said in the strength section. I do not expect you to understand why I felt that way. Why?

Not every one will comprehend what the state of feeling abandoned and being too self-sufficient brings to the table as a single person. That is why! Everybody's conditions are different! That is why! Some people might suffer from a "Fear of being alone condition" where people find themselves just going from relationship to relationship with no breaks in between. Some people might suffer from a "Sex condition" where anything that does not involve a sexual act does not make them feel loved.

Everyone has his/her own weaknesses, which is why you must go through this process to expose that **unhealthy mental state**. You have to know where you stand and BE HONEST ABOUT IT! For you to comprehend where you stand as a single person, you first must be willing to thoroughly evaluate what provided that present state of mind. **(Mission Statement)** Then once you are honest about it, you must be willing to be sincere about correcting it. It is only after you complete those tasks that you become adamant about your **unhealthy mental state** not affecting your personal vision statement any longer.

So here is that opportunity to do it and more! Here is that opportunity to expose what is stopping you from being the person you really want to be and possibly being in the relationship that you dream of being in. Here is your chance to admit, correct and gain direction toward unlocking yet another secret behind being single. Here is your opportunity to be paroled and released from mental bondage! How about we get to writing down some weaknesses now?

Personal Weaknesses

_____

_____

_____

_____

_____

_____

At this very moment, you are owed a resounding applause and congrats! Take a serious look at what you've just written down! Study it! Examine it! More significantly, I want you to pat yourself on the back. The reason is you have just taken a significant step of removing a crutch that you have stood on for so many years of your single life. That is something to be exceedingly proud of right now! You have taken a solemn step toward becoming a better you!

Understand this, as a single person the intentions of your weaknesses were never meant to keep you weak. The intentions were meant to reveal everything within you that prevents you from becoming strong. The intentions were meant to enhance you! The intentions were designed to uncover the obstacles standing in your way! The intentions of your weaknesses are meant to lean you toward accomplishing your vision rather than being stuck in a state of mind that does nothing to contribute to transforming you into your vision.

I want you to know that I am a living witness of what can happen when you learn the definition and purpose of weaknesses. I can state with clarity that admitting and correcting my weaknesses is what gave me direction toward how to love with freedom, which is exactly what my personal vision was as a single person looking to be in a healthy relationship. I am here to tell you that similar results can happen for you as well! All you have to do is be willing and by just being willing you unlock yet another secret behind why you are single! Enjoy the journey of getting to know the real you!

Let's move on to strategy secret #3!

STRATEGY SECRET #3

Let me start this section by telling you to relax. Take a deep breath! You absolutely have nothing to worry about ladies and gentleman. Why? This section has no writing portion in it so you can take a sigh of relief. You do not have to dig any deeper than you already have dug about yourselves. However, there is one caveat! You do have to remember everything that you have written to this point and apply it to what you are about read in this section. That is the only stipulation!

Besides, by the time you finish reading this section and applying the learned information from previous sections, you will understand and thank me for not making you write down anything. Why? For one, I cannot provide you enough writing space to write down all the opportunities that you will begin to spot after reading this section. For two, everybody's list of opportunities will not be identical. Some lists will be longer than others because it will be specifically based on the detail of your personal vision. So, let's just stop talking about it and actually be about it. Let's begin!

To this point, you have been made aware of your real strengths and made conscious of your weaknesses that prevent you from operating within your real strengths! The question now is, "what's next?" The answer is the **Single Person SWOT Analysis** now places you in position for opportunity! The type of opportunity that helps you to experience opportunity as a single person seeking to be in a real relationship; rather than what most of you do, which is seek opportunity to become an opportunist for a relationship. Does that type of opportunity interest you?

Before you answer that question with any answer other than yes, I want to offer you some incentives as to why you should be interested in this type of opportunity. **Incentive one:** you should be interested because you should want to know the type of opportunity that now exist for you due to discovering your real strengths. **Incentive two:** you should be interested because you should want to know, "What exactly does being an opportunist for a relationship mean?" You should be yearning to know, "How have you become an opportunist for a relationship?"

That is the exact epiphany that I hope you are experiencing and exact questions that I hope you are asking. But if not, then let's quickly get on the same page because that is exactly where I need your thought process to accurately comprehend what I am about to tell you. So, first thing first, let's start with the basics, which is what allows you to see opportunity as a single person. Please pay close attention!

Every single person walking this earth has the ability to **see** opportunity for a courting relationship. But for that person to see this opportunity, they must first do two basic things. They must give up and get over! What does that mean? What do you want me to give up and get over?

It means that the first basic thing you need to do is **give up your pride** to properly prepare your heart for the right opportunity. Then after, the second basic thing is **get over your perception** to properly prepare your mind for the right opportunity. To break this down into a much simpler explanation, you must **give up and get over** the very two elements that keep most single people heart's hardened and minds unclear into understanding what a real opportunity for a relationship looks like instead of an opportunity to be an opportunist for one. So, here is breakdown to further help clarify why you must give up and get over.

Why You Must Give Up Pride: What it all boils down to is majority of single people use pride for two reasons. The first reason is to prove something untrue that really is true. The second reason is to protect him/her self from displaying what is believed to be an identical amount of vulnerability shown in a past interpersonal relationship.

Example 1: I have witnessed many single people try their best with trying to prove something does not exist in the initial stages of a courting relationship when in reality it really does exist. (E.g. supreme admiration or fondness for a person)

Example 2: I have witnessed many single people pass on the opportunity to express their emotions to a person during courting once those emotions have elevated to levels beyond expectation. (E.g. graduated feelings of like to love)

Now, let me ask you a question. After reading those examples, did you say to yourself that sounds ridiculous? I truly hope so because not only does it sound ridiculous, it should show you how unpractical and non-beneficial having pride as a leading emotion is for a single person. Pride basically is an empty emotion that produces an empty result, which helps segue into my next point of why you must give it up.

Why You Must Get Over Perception: Whether you are a man or woman, the result of not giving up pride as a single person becomes this unrealistic perception that makes it hard for your mind to comprehend what an actual real opportunity for something good looks like. How? Well, when you are not busy trying to prove something untrue that really is true, then you are sure as hell busy trying to so-call refrain from displaying an identical amount of vulnerability shown in a past interpersonal relationship. Why?

It is because pride has forced you to perceive yourself as what I stated in one of my previous relationship books, which is a courting relationship conspiracy theorist. A courting relationship conspiracy theorist is a single person who assumes that every encounter with someone has a hidden motive or agenda designed to hurt him/her in some capacity or another. That literally becomes your perception as a single person and closes your mind into visualizing what a beneficial opportunity for a relationship resembles. That ladies and gents, is exactly how this pride and perception exchange operates for a single person.

It starts with causing your heart to be unavailable due to pride and primarily ends with your mind lacking clarity due to perception. I honestly believe that you are oblivious to your actions. I also believe that you do not take into consideration two important factors by performing such actions. (1) The valuable time that you waste by sending yourselves through these mental revolving doors of pride and perception. (2) The favorable relationship opportunities being overlooked by you due to your unavailable nature to be open with your heart and unwilling nature to see past what your heart has forced you to believe.

In your mind, you believe that your "cause" for having this pride and perception is somehow helping you; but in actuality you are unconsciously becoming "The Cause" as to why you are unable to see opportunity that a single person should be able to see. And although pride and perception are the main roots as to why you mainly cannot see this opportunity, it ultimately comes down to you simply selecting to worship a paradigm that is not meant for growth as a single person rather than seeing past worthless emotions to create a new one. So Shaun, what are you trying to tell me?

In a nutshell, here is what I am trying to tell you! If you really want to see what real opportunity for a courting relationship as a single person truly looks like, then giving up pride and getting over perception are the prerequisites to get a glance at it. This is just what has to be done to see it. But of course at this stage of being single, I am quite sure you want to go beyond just seeing real opportunity. I am almost confident that you want to experience it as well. So now the questions become, how do I experience it? What do I have to do to experience it? Let's talk about it! Let's talk about how to experience opportunity in the way it is supposed to be experienced. Please, pay closer attention now!

The reason I want you to pay closer attention now is because what I am about to tell you needs your extreme focus. Why? Here is where I attempt to explain to you how most of you have become opportunist for relationships. Here is where I explain to you how most of you have been mishandling the **"Experience"** aspect of opportunity. So lets begin!

Outside of obvious reasons why I want you to give up and get over, which is to see opportunity. The real perspective altering reason as to why I want you to give up and get over is because when you learn how to accurately **see opportunity** as a single person then you learn how to properly **seize opportunity** as a single person. Seize opportunity? What does that mean?

It means this single people! The way in which you seize opportunity as a single person strictly depends on which side of the fence that you unconsciously operate from as a single person. That basically means finding out what rules your train of actions when opportunity is presented to you as a single person for a relationship. Is it your mission **(present state of mind as a single person)** or vision **(what you desire to be as single person)**? Do you seize opportunity based on **weaknesses (Conditions)** or **learned qualities (Elements Chosen to Add to Your Make-up)** or **real strengths (The Foundation of You)**?

Here is a more elaborate way to stress my point! Typically, the only opportunity that you are able to seize when solely operating out of **weaknesses** or **learned qualities** is generally in the form of a come-up. This means that you unconsciously are considering future boy/girl friends or husbands/wives based on the wonderful job a person has done with physically marketing themselves, which ultimately makes them appear more relationship ready. It also means that these particular people have done a good job with speaking to your insecurities as well.

> For example: If you are a single person that has certain weaknesses about yourself then a person that displays a certain learned quality will appeal to you. Now, I know that it was said in the beginning that learned qualities mixed with strengths could make for one hell of an individual. But, one thing you should know is learned qualities mixed with weaknesses can make for one hell of an illusion, which is why I explained in the "Strength Section" that learned qualities alone could not sustain a relationship.

Now, on the flip side of the coin, if your train of actions are being operated from as a single person based on real strengths **(The Foundation of You),** then you are in a much better position to analyze opportunity in a way that helps to recognize if a person has real potential outside of physical benefits. It is in my opinion that a rooted foundation helps you to see through the illusions that many people hide behind and try carrying into relationships that have a way of burdening you in the long run. It also is in my opinion that when you have a full grasp of your identity as an individual, then it helps you get a full view of if a relationship with someone adds the mental, emotional, and spiritual elements that you need added to the mix.

Here is the bottom line point! When you operate out of real strengths then there are more elements taken into consideration rather than just the one most of you believe has enough foundation to hold a relationship together, which is the physical. In essence, what I am trying to say is operating out of your real strengths take you beyond simply concentrating on the physical aspect of a person. It helps you get to the core of that person! It helps you to seize opportunity for a real courting relationship in the way it supposed to be seized. It also helps you seize opportunity in a way that makes you not **plug** someone into your life based on incompleteness. Does that make sense? I hope so because we are about to dive a little deeper into this process!

The reason I want to dive deeper is I want to show you how to recognize which side of you controls your train of actions and ultimately pushes you toward how to seize opportunity. I want to further discuss this **plug** that you use as a temporary fix. In fact, I want to explain to you what a **plug** is and why most of you use it. At this point, I just want to offer you some foreseeability so that you can stay out of hindsight, which in most cases is not 20/20. The reason I say it's not 20/20 is because most of you appear unaware of what's happening around you. Then when you become aware you go into denial because you are not equipped on how to move forward. So basically, it boils down to you simply not possessing the ability to seize opportunity in the right way, which is fine at this point. That is not the concern! The concern here at this particular moment is, "Are you ready to change?" Moreover, will you be ready to seize opportunity no longer as an opportunist once I show you what I am about to show you about this **plug**? We shall see! Let's get started!

__THE PLUG__

What is a plug? During my single days, I often found myself plugging relationships into places of my life that were meant to plug myself into. Here is what I mean! There was certain incompleteness about myself that I was supposed to address myself. There were certain voids within myself that I was supposed to fill myself. The reason I was supposed to perform these tasks myself is because it would have better prepared me for the commitments of a relationship before actually entertaining one. For example:

1. How to commit to becoming more self-disciplined

2. How to commit to becoming more selfless

3. How to commit to learning my self-worth outside of physical attributes and learned characteristics

Basically, just discovering the tools it would have taken to sustain a courting relationship beyond 6 months. But, it was not until later that I discovered the reasons behind me not being able to sustain a courting relationship beyond 6 months. The reasons were as follow: (1) I had not done what I was supposed to in order to see what real opportunity looks like for a single person. (2) By me not doing what I needed to do to accurately see real opportunity, there was no way for me to properly seize it.

Outside of those reasons, I just was not mentally prepared to study my issues as a single person. I really didn't care to commit beyond what was already present. So, instead of dealing with those issues head on, I would see and seize opportunity for a relationship with someone that I felt could immediately benefit what lacked within me during that particular time, which ultimately transformed me into becoming a **"Relationship Opportunist."**

For those of you who have been sleeping under a rock and don't have a clue as to what an opportunist is then let me give you the meaning. The dictionary defines it as, *"a person who exploits circumstances to gain immediate advantage rather than being guided by consistent principles or plans."* Based on that definition, I clearly can say that I was an opportunist. I can stand here today and say that I once took immediate advantage of relationships just to avoid facing the fact that I had no principles in place to guide me or plan on how to gain traction toward accomplishing the envisioned single person I had buried within me. I lacked direction! I had no clue of where to go as a single person looking to be in a relationship. And although it was hard to admit back then, I now can stand in my truth and say it without conviction. The question is, "Can you?"

Can you admit that not being able to accurately see opportunity has caused you to improperly seize it and transform you into a relationship opportunist? I ask that question because if you are unable to admit it now then you will be unable to accurately see and properly seize opportunity as a single person later. You will not be able to take advantage of the prime opportunity that comes with knowing your real strengths as a single person. Not to mention, you will continue to waste time and continue to **plug** relationships into the empty parts of your life. You will just continue to view opportunity as an opportunist, which is sad.

But, there is a light at the end of the tunnel. If you are seriously ready to change your view as a single person, then you are ready to accurately see and properly seize opportunity as a single person. You are prepared to experience single life from a different view, which means we can move on to the next section to discuss the final strategy secret. It also means you are one-step closer to unlocking the huge secret behind being single. So enjoy opportunities as they come now! But make sure you are enjoying them from the side of you rooted in solid foundation! Let's move on to the next phase of the process!

STRATEGY SECRET #4

Here we are at the final undercard before the main event! You have reached the final strategy secret that helps you uncover the huge secret behind being single. I know some of you might be overwhelmed! I know some you might be full of anxiety! I also know some of you might be having a sense of readiness to just get this entire process completed. I wholeheartedly understand your roller coaster of emotions, especially since I had to go through this identical process. But, despite your feeling, you must finish this process strong! You have to continue this journey!

The reasons at this point are very simple and clear! It is just better to be aware than unaware when it comes to being single looking for someone to build and share life with. It is just better to be in position of knowing your true identity as a single person rather than latching onto others to obtain a false sense of one. Lastly, it is just time to grow up and grow out of what you are accustomed to doing as a single person and learn what is specifically catered for you to do. I feel there is no better time for you then now to be where you mainly desire to be as a single person. In fact, consider this section my final plea as to why your real strengths **(The Foundation of You)** are just best for you to operate out of as a single person. Here is a recap of your progress!

Up to this point, you have gained knowledge about your real strengths! You now understand your weaknesses! You now comprehend how to see and seize real opportunity for a courting relationship versus being the opportunist for one. What do you think is the next logical thing that you need to be aware of in order to unlock the huge secret behind being single? What do you think is the last element that stands in your way of becoming the single person you envision to be? The answer is your **THREATS!**

What threats are you talking about? I am talking about the threats that have unconsciously threatened your progress as a single person. Those threats are the final element to reveal that should push you into concentrating more on becoming your **vision** rather than settling in your current **mission**. Those threats are the final element to explain that hopefully will force you to lean more toward appreciating your real **strengths** rather than constantly falling on the sword of your **weaknesses**. Finally, those threats are the final element to expose that should help you understand that threats are a direct result of what comes associated with operating from a current mission that centers around your personal weaknesses and learned qualities without real strengths as the roots.

With that in mind, you should be asking yourself three important questions now: **What are my threats? What is the benefit of knowing my threats? How do I completely let go of my threats?** Luckily, I can help you with answering those questions. But, like the other sections, you have to be open with possibility that what you uncover about yourself is in fact a threat to you as a single person. If you can abide by that one rule, then recognizing the threats that hinder your progress as a single person will be a breeze. So, lets get started with answering that first question!

Question 1: What are my threats?

As previously stated, your threats are the unconscious results gained by acting out of weaknesses, learned qualities, and anything that is not a real strength. The key to discovering these threats rest within your ability to be truthful in evaluating parts of you that has unconsciously caused friction in your past and present courting relationships. That is the underlying factor of figuring out what threatens your progress and prevents you from reflecting your vision statement in present courting relationships as well as future ones. So, there is the root to discovering your threats! My question to you now is, "Are you ready to learn how to pull up that root? If so, how about we use my past threats as an example to help you discover your potential threats?"

In Strategy Secret #2, I told you about my weaknesses. I told you about the impact those weaknesses had on me as a single person in past relationships. However, I really did not provide you with an in-depth example of what came attached with those weaknesses. I did not get the chance to fully explain how those weaknesses threatened me as well as my future courting relationships. I merely gave you some of the effects, but I did not give you the residue that was unconsciously left on me as a single person from those experiences. So lets just start at that point!

If you remember in SS #2, I told you my weaknesses were abandonment and self-sufficiency. Outside of the information that was given to you in that section about my weaknesses, here is a better understanding of the threats that came along with those weaknesses. Here are examples to further show the dangers of solely operating from weaknesses and learned qualities as a single person. **Example 1:** Due to my abandonment weakness, I allowed **neediness** and **clinginess** to become apart of me as a single person. I also allowed it to become a threat to future courting relationships. **Example 2:** As for my self-sufficient weakness, I allowed **inconsideration** and **belittling** to become the threat to me as a single person and future courting relationships. But, let me further explain myself!

Neediness and clinginess became the direct result of my abandonment condition because I ultimately felt self-entitled. I assumed that since I felt abandoned as a single person, it was up to my partner to step up to the plate and help me feel less abandoned in a relationship. But, by having such thoughts, I had never taken into consideration how much of a threat placing that type of responsibility on my partner could be to my courting relationships or to me personally. The same goes for inconsideration and belittling. The only difference in this case was those feelings were the direct results of arrogance. My imbalanced self-sufficient condition threatened my courting relationships and me as a single person because I was either being too inconsiderate by doing things without consulting my partner or belittling my partner for not being able to do things in the manner that I saw fit.

Now, keep that in mind as we take a slight turn toward the learned qualities aspect of this scenario. In fact, I mentioned in a previous section about listening being one of my learned qualities, but I did not go into detail about the other ones. So outside of listening, I also picked out providing to be a learned quality as well. Now, here was the downfall!

Without real strengths associated to use with those learned qualities in the right way, the only thing I actually learned was **how to listen to manipulate** and how to **provide without substance**. Ultimately, that meant the threats to me as a single person and future courting relationships were knowing how to **manipulate** people for what I wanted and **providing** those people with whatever was needed to get whatever was wanted at that particular time.

For the sake of this conversation, let's just say that my personal progress as a single person was multi-threatened. Let's also say that my courting relationships were in the same boat as well. But, that is enough about me. Let's get back to focusing on you, which is the purpose of this section and book. Now that my threats are on the table for all to see, what do you think I want you to do next? Yes, you have guessed it! You have to write your threats down! You have to put a list together! You have to view that list word by word and let it marinate what could potentially be costing you plenty of courting relationships with more than qualified candidates.

But before you do that, take a peep at my list to visualize what I need from you at this particular stage of the section!

Shaun D. Upshaw's Threats
Neediness
Clinginess
Self-Entitlement
Inconsideration
Belittling
Arrogance
Manipulation
Providing With No Substance

Here is a question for you! Do you see the ugliness of that list? I dare you to search and define each of those words! If the definitions alone do not make you cringe, then clearly this book has not had any pull on you to this point. But if it does, can you now understand why those were considered threats? This list is just an example of what you unconsciously might be allowing to threaten your single person's progress. This merely is a reference point of what might be threatening you from operating out of your real strengths as a single person. But enough with the assumptions and speculations, the question is, "Are you ready to take a crack at finding out?"

At this point, I truly hope so because if you've reached this level of the process, then you are ready. So, let's take advantage of this opportunity to learn more about self? All you have do at this moment is just recall the weaknesses that you written down about yourself in the previous section, then dig deep to recall the unconscious actions that might have come associated with those conditions. The same applies for those learned qualities without real strengths as the roots! Remember this process is to help you! But, in order to get that help, it means you have to be ready to accept opportunities for help! Let's get to writing!

Your Threats

Now that your potential threats are written down, I want you to take a serious look at that list. Not only should you be proud of yourself for uncovering those threats, but you also should be excited to finally be able to have an accurate evaluation of the last element possibly threatening you from moving to the next level as a single person. You clearly can now recognize your unconscious actions and take action toward getting rid of those stagnant characteristics about you. Congrats! Let's move on to answering the next question!

Question 2: What is the benefit of knowing my threats?

My mantra once my threats became visible was "Now that I'm able to see it, I am more than able to neutralize it." I know that sounds a bit corny, but that mantra has a benefit in it. Matter of fact, it is the benefit that will make you one dangerous individual. The reason I can offer you that type of accolade is because once my threats did become recognizable, it gave me a sense of **awareness and readiness,** which in turn prepared me for the attacks that came my way as a result of knowing my threats. Attacks?

Yes! Attacks! But, let me give you exact detail into what I am trying to explain here. The one aspect regarding my threats that I often found interesting was they always seem to know the very moment I was not intimidated by them any longer. I know that sounds strange, but hear me out before judgment. It was as if my threats had the timing and power to pull me back into operating out of my weaknesses and learned qualities without strengths as the roots. It was almost as if when I made the decision to no longer allow my threats to be an issue for me as a single person, that a variety of situations would arise before me, which during that particular time if I was operating out of anything outside of real strengths could be considered prime opportunity to act as an opportunist single person.

But, that's where the **awareness and readiness** came into the fold. By being aware, I was able to see what was happening. By being ready, I was able to apply actions to prevent the threat from happening. So basically, I am telling you that the key benefit of knowing your threats is having a sense of **awareness and readiness** to know the times that you are being tempted to revert to a negative state of mind. However, that benefit does not present itself viable until you have completed your first task, which is accurately and honestly acknowledging your threats.

The only way you can discover if your threats have been accurately and honestly acknowledged is by your reactions to those moments in which threaten you to be pulled in the opposite direction of your vision. Then and only then is when that benefit activates to push you away from being a single person that you know is not you. In other words, this benefit is fundamentally the good angel that tells the bad angel its presence is no longer needed because your vision requires nothing less than your real strengths to operate in as a single person. Case closed! Lets move on to final question!

Question 3: How do I completely let go of my threats?

The answer to this question is much more easier than you think people! The reason is because the hard parts are out of the way. You have acknowledged the threats and followed that by attaining the benefit of knowing your threats! All that's left now is the next step of simply making a decision. What it comes down to is you must choose to no longer allow your threats to be threats to your single progress and future courting relationships. You must choose to no longer allow your weaknesses as well as learned qualities without real strengths being the roots to lead your way of thinking and doing as a single person.

If you feel that anything I am asking you to do at this point is not easy, then clearly the notion of being stagnant outweighs the realization of you becoming your vision. In essence, that is the truth of the matter. You simply must be comfortable with failing in your courting relationships. I say that with confidence because there is no other way to view someone that now knows what threatens his/her potential to be great and the benefit of being great; but still chooses not to release the threats. There is no other explanation to put in place to justify such behavior.

So, do us both a favor, just admit that you are comfortable with your threats. Admit that operating out of weaknesses and learned qualities has afforded you a current mission to be able to manipulate, mentally abuse, and use other poor qualities that permit you to remain in your present identity. If that is where you want to stay, then by all means stay! I am not trying to be harsh or anything, but some times the truth is the truth. Some times the truth cannot be presented in a way that is appetizing. The ugliness of it just has to be brought out to the light for you to step out of hiding in the dark.

But sarcasm aside, if you really want change in your behavior as a single person, then the decision of letting go of your threats is easy. The decision is not only easy, but it also is blatantly visible as to why you should make it. When you get right down to it, this decision determines the fate of whether you will become the envisioned single person that you desire to be or remain the stagnant single person most of you are right now. Now what person do you really want to be? That ultimately is the question here! I want you to seriously think about it before moving to the next section, which reveals the huge secret behind being single.

The reason is because if you not sure of who you want to be, then everything done to this point will be viewed in vain. Everything will be considered a waste of time. Nothing discovered about you up this point will be truly appreciated. But more important, you will miss out on becoming the single person that I know you desire to be and have envisioned to become at some point. Don't allow confusion to stop the process! Let those threats completely go! Learn the huge secret behind why you are single! Turn the page!

THE HUGE SECRET

If you have reached this point of the book, then evidently there are aspects about this process that has driven you to want to discover the huge secret behind being single. There are aspects about this process that has revealed some truths about you as a single person as well. So in other words, this process has done exactly what I set out for it to do, which is push you to embrace the true identity of you. Not only do I respect the fact that you have submitted to those aspects, but I am also proud of you for doing what it took to learn beyond what you believed to be the reason behind being single. Now, how about one last recap of your amazing progress?

To this point, you have familiarized yourself with your real strengths **(Foundation of You)**. You have realized the definition and purpose behind your weaknesses/conditions. You have made the decision to see and seize opportunity in the correct way rather than the opportunist way. Last, you have reached an understanding of the threats associated with operating outside of the foundation of who you truly are as a single person. I must say that without a doubt those are learning points to be extremely proud of and here is why!

Do you recall all that unpleasant digging and writing that I had you to do about yourself? I am sure you do! As a matter of fact, I think some of you still might be upset with the fact that I had you do it, which I can understand. However, here is where all that hard work pays off. Here is the moment when you piece together your masterpiece! Here is where you become impressed by your work! But like I have done throughout this entire book, let me show you my masterpiece first so that you can be just as impressed by yours as I was with mine once I finished this process. Take a look at this people! Check out the purpose behind your digging and why you should be extremely proud!

Personal Guide
Personal Mission Statement: To get everything I want out of a relationship without giving anything in return that places me in a position of vulnerability, hurt, and/or brokenness.

Personal Vision Statement: To become a person who can love someone in freedom! Freedom from past hurts! Freedom from brokenness! Freedom from bitterness! Freedom from unforgiveness! Freedom from self-sabotaging! Freedom from victimization! Freedom from familiarity (Characteristics that were inherited from my parent's relationship experiences)

Personal SWOT Analysis

Real Strengths: Individuality, Loyalty, and Unconditional Love

Learned Qualities: Listening, Providing

Weaknesses/Conditions: Abandonment, Self –Sufficiency

Opportunities: Marriage, Children, Love, Stability, Etc.

Threats: Neediness, Clinginess, Self-Entitlement, Inconsideration, Belittling, Arrogance, Manipulation, Providing With No Substance

For those of you confused by what you just read, let me give you an explanation. I just provided you with everything that I once was as a single person and everything that I transformed into as a single person. But, here is a more meticulous breakdown to explain what I am trying to show you. Here was the difference between me operating from the root of a mission **(Present State of Mind)** vs. a vision **(Where You Want To Be)** as a single person. Pay attention!

Left me with Neediness, Clinginess, Self-Entitlement, Inconsideration, Belittling, and Arrogance as threats to my progress as a single person and future courting relationships

Caused my learned qualities to be Listening to manipulate and Providing to only get what I ultimately wanted in return

Left me susceptible to thinking as a single person based on the weaknesses/conditions of "Abandonment and Self-Sufficiency"

Root: To get everything I want out of someone without giving anything in return that places me in a position of vulnerability, hurt, and/or brokenness.

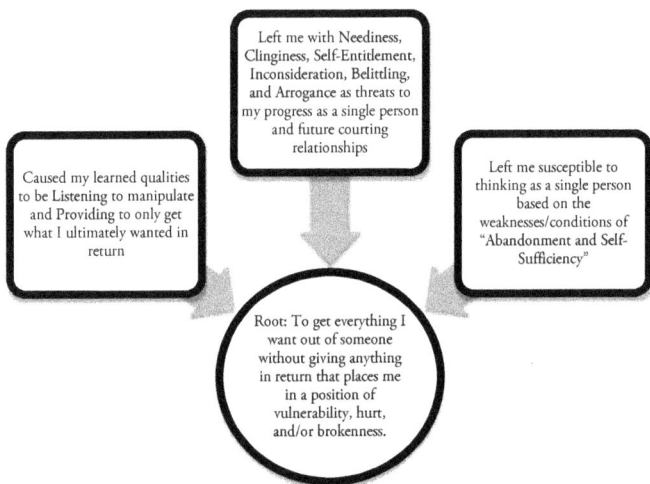

Based on that chart, you can see when my mission **(Present State of Mind)** as a single person was the root of my train of thoughts, then nothing good came as a result of it. There was nothing that offered a ray of hope that one day I could find a long lasting relationship. It was all about how I felt at that particular time about my singleness and what I can gain from others without giving up anything about myself. As you can see, there was nothing in place that held me accountable for my actions, nor responsible for the way I treated my opportunities to change. I basically had succumbed to allowing my mission **(Present State of Mind)** to be my guiding principles as a single person. Why?

It is because I wanted to be the victim of past relational circumstances. I did not want to forgive those who had wronged me. Hell, I did not want to forgive myself for allowing myself to be wronged by others. I just wanted to so-call control my outcome by any means necessary, which is what a lot of you try doing with your present state of mind. It does not matter who gets hurt in the process or gets caught up in your web of mess as long as the feeling of a controlled outcome feels present to you. But, here is something that you should know about being that way. In the end, it's all fool's gold because the outcome you really desire does not come from a mentality rooted in chaos. The outcome you truly desires come through being who you have a vision to be as a single person.

It was not until I grew tired of that foolish way of thinking and acting that I decided to create and chase after the vision **(Where I Wanted To Be)** rather than the mission. It was not until I seen myself by myself due to my piss poor mentality that I chose to uncover the truth about who I really wanted to become as a single person. From there, it was a no brainer to make up in my mind that having a vision of where I wanted to be as a single person outweighed the focus of where I was at that particular moment. Not only that, but I just grew tired of hiding behind layers of false identity. I was fed up with operating as a single person that was created from experiences rather than the true roots of a solid foundation. And to this day, I am glad to have made that decision! Check out chart for what happens when the roots of your vision are in the right place!

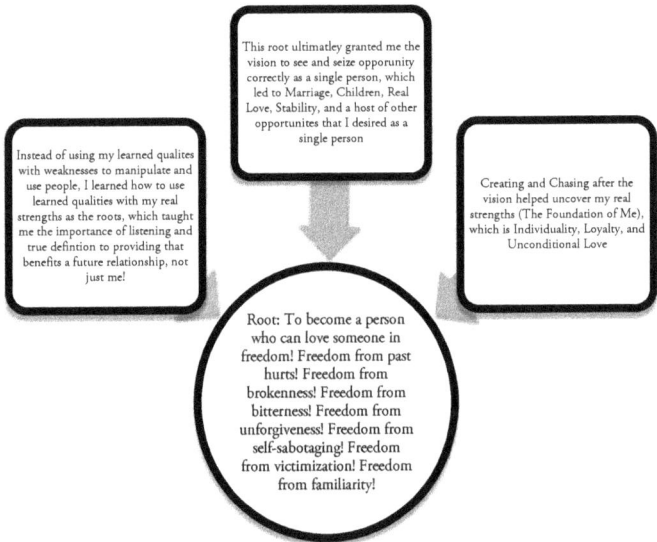

This root ultimatley granted me the vision to see and seize opporunity correctly as a single person, which led to Marriage, Children, Real Love, Stability, and a host of other opportunites that I desired as a single person

Instead of using my learned qualites with weaknesses to manipulate and use people, I learned how to use learned qualities with my real strengths as the roots, which taught me the importance of listening and true defintion to providing that benefits a future relationship, not just me!

Creating and Chasing after the vision helped uncover my real strengths (The Foundation of Me), which is Individuality, Loyalty, and Unconditional Love

Root: To become a person who can love someone in freedom! Freedom from past hurts! Freedom from brokenness! Freedom from bitterness! Freedom from unforgiveness! Freedom from self-sabotaging! Freedom from victimization! Freedom from familiarity!

Based on the information in those charts, you clearly can see the difference in my thinking and actions when the right roots were in place to guide me. In fact, this has been my consistent message throughout every page of this book. I have been trying to get you to understand that the roots of your thinking and actions have to be in the right place for you to understand your true purpose behind being single. But, that is not the only reason your roots have to be in the right place. You ultimately must have your roots in the right place with regards to thinking and acting because you need to know that one of the huge secrets behind being single is to gain the **freedom to change your mission at any given time**.

Yes, you read that correctly! One of the huge secrets behind being single is gaining the **freedom to change your mission at any given time**. I say that because the mission of you as a single person should never be stuck on set experiences with people in previous relationships, past circumstances that are out of your control, and the fear to simply be unapologetically you despite the outcomes of situations.

When you have the **freedom to change your mission at any given time,** then you gain the abilities to accomplish your vision. Having the **freedom to change your mission at any given time** is what always keeps you in position to grow not only as a single person, but also in future courting relationships as well. How? Well, one thing you must understand is that missions in life are designed to be interchangeable, especially missions regarding you as a single person and future courting relationships. The reason is because as you grow as a single person, then so should the vision, which is why you should chase after the vision and allow the mission to center around what is needed to achieve that vision.

It does not get any simpler to explain ladies and gentleman. Your vision is basically the lifeline that saves you, elevates you and places you wherever you desire to be as a single person looking to grow into an individual ready for a worthwhile relationship. It is focusing on your vision that allows you to do the work that needs to be done as an individual entity before trying to partner with someone else to build anything. In a nutshell, if you do not create and chase after your vision as a single person, then you are going to create and leave behind chaos in every courting relationship that you step foot in. Now lets move on to the next huge secret behind you being single.

Outside of gaining the **freedom to change your mission at any given time**, the next huge secret behind being single is to **get the timing right of when you should be released into dating and relationships**. This timing aspect was touched on briefly in the opening pages of the book, but not in full detail. The reason timing is such a significant aspect is because you do not want to miss out on your future Mrs. or Mr. Right.

Have you seen what happens to a product when it is prematurely released? People do not find a use for it! People undervalue its worth! People just flat out ignore that product exists, which basically causes the company to shelf a product that could have revolutionized the market. The same happens with you as a single person when you do have the timing right of when you should be released into dating and relationships.

You do not find a use for patience, so you rush into anything that appears beneficial. You undervalue your worth, which causes you to just get into dating and relationship situations with shallow people who undervalue their worth as well. Last, you just flat out ignore the real foundations of you, which are the elements that primarily set you apart from the rest. You basically shelf the very thing that teaches you that relationships are meant to compliment you, not complete you! And this all happens because you refuse to **get the timing of when you should be released into dating and relationships right**. My question to you at this point is, "How has that worked out for you thus far?"

Don't even bother answering that question. Lets just move on to the last huge secret behind being single, which is really no secret at all. Why? It is because we have been doing it this entire time, which is **learning every part of you that is good, bad, and ugly.** I briefly wrote about this earlier in the book, but now it is time to elaborate on it. **Learning every part of you that is good, bad, and ugly** is a huge secret behind being single because this entire strategy was purposed for you to get a better look at YOU! This entire process was for you to shake the speculation of who you think you are and get down to the core of really finding it out. This process was primarily to show you why you really might be single instead of using assumptions to create a false reality of why.

I cannot stress enough how tired I grow from hearing people say, "I cannot find anyone because there are no good men or women out there." That is such bullshit for lack of a better word! I know for a fact that there are great people out here! However, the reason you could not find them was because you were never in position to see them. You were just unaware of what you unconsciously were doing to keep them away from you. But that is over now! You have the ability to correct that way of thinking now.

Of course, I am not saying that this book has given you all the answers, but I really feel like it has been a perfect tool for you to find the answers. I really feel like if you dug deep within yourself as I asked and taken this process seriously, then you are amazed by what you found out about yourself right now. I feel like you have the building blocks to transform into who you desire to be now. It could be me just over feeling myself as the author, but I feel like this process has helped you open your eyes. I feel like it has helped you change your perspective on being single.

But if not, then I can at least stand behind knowing that this process helped me. It helped me live as the single person I was destined to become. But more significantly, it has placed me in the perfect relationship. The type of perfect relationship that is perfect for me to grow in instead of the perfect relationship for my insecurities to benefit from ladies and gents! Isn't that the type relationship that you want? Guess it all depends on your desires!

Nevertheless, I thank you for taking this journey all the way to the finish line. I pray that learning the huge secrets of **freedom to change your mission at any given time, getting the timing right of when**

you should be released into dating and relationships, and l**earning every part of you that is good, bad, and ugly** has pushed you to want to stay single long enough to get it right. I hope that you will never look at being single as anything other than an opportunity to be the best you. More important, I cross my fingers in faith that this book has given you enough hope to stop operating as a single person from anything that is not the true foundation of YOU!

God Bless You!

Signed,
Shaun D. Upshaw

www.ingramcontent.com/pod-product-compliance
Lightning Source LLC
Chambersburg PA
CBHW061957040426
42447CB00010B/1790